SIMON COCKLE

River Lane

ARENIG PRESS

First published in 2018
by Arenig Ltd (Arenig Press)
Dolfawr, Cwmrheidol, Aberystwyth SY23 3NB

Printed in UK by
4Edge Ltd, 22 Eldon Way, Hockley SS5 4AD

A CIP record for this book
is available from the British Library

ISBN : 978-1-9998491-2-2

Cover: Wiltshire Landscape (1937)
by Eric Ravilious (1903-1942)

IM Fell English font digitally reproduced by Igino Marini.
www.iginomarini.com

Acknowledgements

I would like to thank the editors of the following papers, magazines and e-zines for first publishing some of these poems :

IOTA, Dreamcatcher, The Lampeter Review, Skylight 47, Pantheon, Heron Tree, The Compass Magazine, Picaroon, Three Drops from a Cauldron, the Ledbury Poetry Festival website, In Between Hangovers, The London Progressive Journal, Ink, Sweat and Tears

and the following anthologies:

'Paper Cuts' (Poetry ID, 2016)
'Waiting for the Echo' (Poetry ID, 2017)
'Loosened Threads' (Poetry ID, 2018)
'Secrets and Dreams' (Hurricane Press, 2016)
'The Physic Garden' (Palewell Press, 2017)

Simon was invited to read at the Ledbury Poetry Festival in 2016 and 2017. He won the Wax Poetry and Art Poetry Competition in 2017.

Many thanks to:

John Cockle
Susanne, Anouska and Mum
Martin Evans
John Gohorry
Adam Horovitz
Poetry ID
Dr Johnson

'Memory Cento' contains elements of the following texts: the recipe for dressing a calf's head in American Cookery by Amelia Simmons (1796), the story of "The Three Cows" in More English Fairy Tales by Joseph Jacobs and John D. Batten (1893) and a passage on memory and the brain from Curiosities of Medical Experience by J. G. Millingen (1839).

Contents

River Lane

Vellum

When I arrived,
after one more dismal three-hour drive,

you stood at the door
and stretched out your hand,

made of garlic-paper skin,
to clasp mine.

I saw, inked in red
ballpoint, my first name

in the delta between
your thumb and forefinger.

It was a comfort to know
you remembered me,

written, as I was,
into the parchment of you.

Beachlands, Hayling Island

I

You hold tight the memories you wish to keep;
you discard the rest like knots in handkerchiefs.

So the plastic afternoons
of my childhood,
spent cross-legged in wet trunks
on the flea-peppered beach
at Hayling Island,
become a fairy-tale of ice-cream
and Black Forest castles as
the sun splinters,
crystalline, on the ridges
of slow-motion breakers.

I throw smooth, patterned stones at the waves;
only noise and filth are returned at my feet.

2

Close season; snow settles
in for the night as the sun,
whose journey above the horizon
had barely begun, lies low
behind its sleeve of water.

The beach has gone;
under this covering
of pale slush, it attracts
no one. Even the dogs
of winter feign interest.

2

Drifts collect in the shelter
of tarred groynes, making dunes
around derelict castles with
their shed-feather flags
and cigarette butts for soldiers.

Other flakes fall on the slate
face of the sea - their fractals
make little impression;
in the moment they present,
they are nothing again.

3

My father and mother met on this beach;
they parted company here,
when half a century had passed.

There were no words then; the sea
had more to say that April morning.

A scattering of ashes, and she was returned
to the whale-deep of the echoing ocean.
She loved its sound, its promise;

now, I hear her rush of excitement
in the constancy of her waves.

Wheat Field in July

We walked a field of wheat,
                    a sea of teeth,
that slid away from the sky
down to the valley stream,
                    dry now as the husks
it might once have served.

We made a line, straight as sunlight,
                    cut plumb
between the kneeling stalks
while tiny mouths breathed the sun,
                    holding it in,
waiting for a sign to exhale.

Beneath, cool shadows collected
                    where mice ran,
drunk, through the dust,
and flint shone purple amongst
                    bits of brick,
old nails, gone seed and rent bone.

A few lost stalks stood in our way.
                    Golden and blue/green,
they looked the same
though separation made
                    lepers of them;
they offered no resistance.

Black clouds from the west brought rain
                    and thoughts of home.
We made our way to where
the hedge crested the hill
                    and, turning back,
we could see where we had come from.

The Shire Horse

It was the vast cock that stopped me in my tracks;
unfurling slowly downwards, like a flesh telescope.
That, and the height; seventeen hands high,

wreathed in clouds of steam in the freezing air.
Then the hooves, like plinths, that welded him
to the stable floor. He was *fit for the dray*, alright;

I stood in terror, taking in the arch of black neck
to the mane that hung like witches' hair. The eye,
bone-white, glaring through a claw of lashes.

Then I was away, past crowds of open mouths.
All that day, I checked for his shadow.

Kingfisher

Deep in the midst of a circular walk,
we forded the stream that runs
past the meadow. I caught you
first; it was luck, as always.

Furled on a knuckle of hawthorn,
eye bandaged white like a campaign
reminder - a kingfisher, gathering.
You scanned your jungle of possibilities,

a drillbit bolted to a castellation
of feathers, bruised orange and blue;
imperial. Nothing escaped you.
A cartwheel of wings and you darted

left. The river seemed to flow
backward as you sped through
the evening vacuum; the bullrushes
bent in your wake, inquisitive.

You fell as if speared but, rising,
I saw, in your rude tapering of bone,
the spent silver of a dead perch.
In seconds, we saw it throated

whole. You did the same to time
and space; telescoped, concertinaed,
while we stood on the bank, our hands
in our pockets, rooted, as always.

River Lane

I

From the main road at a right-angle runs
River Lane - twin-furrowed, tree-lined.

In a matter of yards, it narrows to
a fog of shadows. The willows cave in

on themselves and the lane is a tunnel
to the slow river. I see myself now

as a child, all taught and imagination
in my new coat and scarf, walking

down to where men sought the pulse
of fish, disgorged hooks from lips.

I beat the paths behind these anglers,
eyes scanning each detail like a spy.

I knew of their straining creels, floats
and spoons, line and split-shot

that rattled as they paced the swim
and planted their rests, hands in pockets.

I watched for signs of maleness - the clasped
cough that cigarettes gave them - and those

maggots that bristled, churned bronze
like simmered rice; a million ribbed

muscles, beating their carrion tattoo
in an orgy of silence. For eyes, full stops.

But the men looked on, reading the currents
for bubbles, a spasm of fin or mouth,

the red bob of the bite, the take, the run
with the bait that draws the *Perch,*

Dace, Chubb and *Bream* - the common
currency of the English river in season.

They charmed the fish from the lush
throat of the course. They squatted,

struck like pulled piano wire and
lifted hooked fish up past 'rushes,

'cress gluts, *Brooklime* and *Celandine,*
the *Cuckooflower* or *Lady's Smock,*

hovered above the *Cleaver*'s
hooked stickiness like a scaled tear,

over *Marshmallow, Saxifrage, Samphire,*
Meadowsweet, Ribwort and, there,

into the keep net - a possession of sorts.
I ran back up the lane to meet my mates

and hear their noise, the words that showed
like badges, flags or collections of stamps.

2

There, we picked our way down the lane;
a murder of boys, with our sticks and our mouths
declaiming *'Spurs*, or some new best name,
to each other and what stood for clouds.

Through a hedge-gap at random, we'd pass
into dense, thick-sprung tangles of branches
and emerge into clearings at last.
And there, sagged in wrinkled bunches,

the refuse sacks, fly-tipped or hidden.
Spilling out of some black crack like fish scale,
we saw the coloured gloss first. Then, suddenly,
the rushing pulse like hammering nails

that told we'd found porn mags in bin bags.
We descended like flies and tore at the plastic.
Each took one, repairing to some private edge,
in pairs or alone, like some vivid electric

dream. *Escort, Penthouse* - the titles lettered
and formed like a wink. They were saloon cars,
aftershaves, driving gloves, golf clubs; the street-light
iconography of manhood as font. We lifted the covers.

Our nervousness made us tremble. My mouth formed
a Q-shape, my hands shook with hay-fever as we started
to leaf through the pages. Here were stories called
She Can't Stop, Afternoon with Lucy and *Tart*.

And there, unmistakable pull-down of focus, the form
of a naked woman. She sat at a dressing table;
she undressed. The man was poised behind her, calm.
Then, together, we began the oldest game.

As maps have their codes and contours, so
the swollen tangle of hair, member and limb
showed a landscape of desire; the ebb and flow,
a contraction of space, a topography of skin.

He was there, with teeth and a tongue, where she
yawned a bruise and, next picture, she returned
to where his piss came and, last page, her scream
of joy like the flesh screw of a Chinese burn.

Each picture was a new knot: here, one to hold
tight where the loop slid down to bight and turn;
another, where the standing end slipped, rolled
around the working part. They made the *Turk*,

the *Hitch*, the *Figure-of-Eight* and every trick
to which the human form could bend. We sat, hard.
We dared to think ourselves amongst the thick
of it, and pictured (but couldn't say) the word

fuck; these images - the word made flesh -
felt as such. We ran our 'tips across the damp
and slipping ink, connecting with the word. A rash
of print showed, purple, in our hands.

The shriek of a tyre and we were away, with our fingers
sparking and eyes sparking, a fervour to share
with each other, with no-one, with animals, strangers.
Next day, we came back to find them still there.

But the rain had been heavy and the river had swollen up
through the table. Our sacks now held eruptions of pulp
like gluts of tissue. We glanced and saw a nipple, but
nothing else we could comprehend. I felt old,

my age became apparent to me then; I knew that this
was growing up and into something else. It was despair -
for what I couldn't say. But then I knew, at once, it
was the thing I couldn't say that had put me here.

3

Thirty years gone, and the furrows run deeper.
There's a golf course now where the clearing was;

a sand hazard's sunk like a spent blister right
in the place we unearthed those magazines.

Once, we were free to associate. Now
you're trespassing here unless you've got clubs.

The lane still ends at the river; anglers, stagnant,
standing in camouflage, playing the line.

It's late, and rainclouds strain the last of the sun.
The men dismantle rigs and clear the pitch

for leaving. Last of all, the keep net, moored
in the bank, where carp and eels pause.

A heavy hand reaches in, the studied grasp
and silent return. The fish pause and gulp;

they suck the water through and seem stone
dead, but churn and flip and slip slowly down

to the bed again. You thought they never would,
they pantomime so to keep us on hooks.

The river now, at sunset, wears the grey of darkness.
Packed up, the fishermen are set for leaving;

we all have homes to go to, now. Mine's due south;
there's a wife and daughter waiting there, safe,

in the world beyond childhood. Fishing for keys,
I stop, reflect and consider this: what dream

of me will surface in that lane when turning
back to glance at what was left behind?

Loosely-Coupled Systems

(after 'Rich in Vitamin C' by J.H. Prynne)

You said we were like *syrup in a cloud* -
the last spark of the evening sun had arced
pleasantly across the window pane.

We heard the loudness of traffic changing gear
while the leaves rustled, arthritically.
It did us no good; I could not compute

your words. You left in a frenzy of gestures
and I sat where I always sit, imagining sweetness,
trapped by a blur of water vapour, high

above us; a stasis barely held together
with consensus and gravity. That was us,
all over, was it not?

Love Lock

A red padlock reflects
the sun under a blue sky,
fixed to the safety mesh

of a four-lane bridge.
The Danube moves east
below, slow as words,
around the bow.

An inscription - *Wenzel
loves Julia* (paired hearts);
sealed with a hand, romantic
and machine-precise.

Who put it there - him or her -
and are they still together,
an item in a coffeehouse
somewhere across town?

The key may lie, concealed,
in a warm coat pocket
or dragging the riverbed.

Incident by the Seine

A crowd had paused on the bridge,
the one before the artist's row, the prints
and academic French paperbacks. We stopped
to focus on the quay beside a green barge.
Frowning men examined the churning grey
below. A drowning or a capsized ship?
The air reduced to whispers and cameras
scanned the scene to catch what was to come.
Then we saw a spasm of movement; a flash
of hip-flask silver that took the river with it.
A man backed up the steps to much applause,
dragging a monstrous catfish by its mouth,
and flopped, exhausted, on the concrete bank,
too rapt with all to know why he was here.

Aubrey

His hands are wired, pocked;
the tin bones fused with years
of clenched fists, hard skin.

He stands on my doorstep
holding a teardrop; a sock
with a billiard ball in the toe.

Somewhere, the shark's teeth
of the Swiss Alps surface.
How did you end up, here,

clutching that thing? I ask.
Holding my eyes, he says:
We got in my sports car

*after work on a Friday
and were in Neuchâtel
by lunch the next day.*

Lincoln

'Lincoln has been named as the UK city which experiences the most road rage'
Lincolnshire Echo, July 10th, 2015

My face
has touched
the surface of the sun.

It is
the deranged tattoo
of every wasp
captured in a jar.

My face
is a balled fist,
steeped in the brine
of sweat.

It frames
a mouth of concrete;
the teeth will disintegrate
before the contents.

This is
my face, now,
imprinted
on the windscreen -
the face
I offer you.

Gamekeeper

He could set traps   to catch rabbits
but his double bed   was seldom full.
With his rusty shotgun   and silver flask,
he would track strides   from hidden setts,
read shadows   and taste the breeze.
But his keen mind,   when tasked with affection
and the sport of love,   would fail to open
or else snap shut   on nothing but air;
he could catch their eye   but not their hearts.
With his French Gin   now carefully prepared,
he can kill time   in the dead of night
with foolish thoughts   of a certain girl
and trapping her   all for himself.

Maypole

they sing themselves around the maypole
                those girls who thread and mingle in the Spring
electric strands of reds, whites and blues
                meander in and out of each other, weaving patterns
above their heads, held in orbit, threatening
                to cut free, to fling themselves into outstretched arms
now see the grass they beat down with their feet
                and the stalk will not bend but the tree is supple
and I wished it, willed it so - only then
                look away beyond the hill past strip lynchets
and the hung white bands of electric fences
                and hedges that fall away to the field's edge
proceed to the water meadows thick with exhaust
                and cheap maisonettes anointed with spilt beer broken
doors where the May Queen hides her bruise
                as the stream is sluggish and drags last year's leaves
across its bed of scum and rusted pitchforks, oh
                Jesus would not wish to walk upon this brackish water
he may choose the bridle path instead but suddenly
                sirens from the past triple echo us back
to the church and the sunken thatched cottages
                like wet loaves that rose then fell back sapped
where night has drowned the village green and
                the maypole stands arrayed in spent colours
a dusting of elderflower frost and the girls
                will ravel up the ribbons to be packed away
in tea chests under the stage in the village hall

                with the flags   the eyelashes   the silence

Tumulus

Run your fingertip across a map
and feel the dead swell.

Search for the fallen star: it marks
a grave, a tumulus.

Walk it for real and all you'll find
is the ghost of a mound,

ploughed in thick with flints and roots;
the grave goods robbed,

spent with the wet flesh and hair years ago.
You might turn a bone,

snag a tooth, or leave with an offering:
a shudder that sets the flesh

pricking. You can turn back now,
but the mark was made.

Escapement

Grandfather's pocket watch
stopped this morning.

It stalled on the mantelpiece
in its hammered silver case,
the ivory face and hands,
stuck at twenty past eight,
pointing to the British Empire.

Dad wound it up again
so we could hear the cogs
and gears of the past
grinding in the corridors
of memory. Peering

around a door, I saw
a yew tree bending over
a gravestone strewn
with petals turned to ash.

Hartland Point

In the tides of the night,
time folds
like an origami bird
and, perched on the windowsill,
describes an ornament;
nothing more.

I lie still, but
keep my arm straight
up in the dark air,
answering a question
that's not yet been asked.
The mind, however, needs

diversions like these;
sleep is the trick of catching a sneeze,
the balancing act between
death and waking,
the clench of toes
at the edge of a skyscraper.

Meanwhile,
in a dream
in someone else's head,
the *May Queen* borrows and
fetches in the swell
around Hartland Point.

Negatives

Shadows lengthen on the lawn
now summer's here. Dead leaves have gone
to earth or turned to dust. Blue skies
replace Spring's palette of ashen greys.
And, all because the earth's renewed,
my childhood memories unspool;
the long-ago, in dark rooms, form
by liquid night and chemical gloom.
They float, fix, softly at first
until the souls of years past
appear in sunshine, black as slate.
With careful fingers, I present
the negatives of yesterday
to light that scares the ghosts away.

The Matlock Holograms

Where the river bends through Matlock Dale
and the fish shops thin to a file of office blocks,
there's an exhibition of holograms. You follow

signs through the Old Bath House; a maze
of aquaria, a poolful of sherbet-coloured Koi;
and the spring that petrifies all it drowns.

You enter their room and, at once, they flaunt
their lashes beneath a gauze of laser light.
They glow green, with the faces of mannequins,

caught in stasis but, close-up, it's a pantomime
they present; a karaoke of movement,
an empty beckoning. It's you

that brings them to life; there's nothing
behind them. The clock parts, the puzzles
and waxwork faces that glow like chlorophyll,

half in love with the trick of it. They're screwed
to the wall should they grab your shoulders,
affect an escape, or pull you by the throat

into their hermetic undersea cave.
They stupefy the weak and uninitiated
but it's just front; they're simply not all there.

When leaving, you glance back and return
their dumb gaze. They continue performing
to ghosts; their audience is each other, now.

Head Transplant

I am the pilot
cockpit of bone
frozen Gepetto
your string-puller

body was kindling so
they counted me
into unconsciousness
severed the cord

anti-bodies rushed
my woven tissue
gristle and muscle
Frankenstein stitching

but our cells meshed
reproduced reproduced
and made a rose of
our scar tissue

now I fit my arms
inside your arms
my pumpkin head
carrot nose coal for eyes

locked on your spine
my nod's my own but
my hand is not my hand
I touch ourself in horror

Rooks on a Pylon

Descending
from the corner of my eye,
higher than clouds, wheeling like leaves,
offering a wingful, then settling
to cawing like mooncalves:

a traffic of rooks, perched
amongst the volts.

Up here,
their world is curved
into an eye; beaks trace lines
on the ground, scratching maps
in their fleet minds for later.

For now, they are gods
in a pantheon of girders.

A crackle
of blue and the rooks
scatter like ash from a bonfire,
vaulting downwards for more
black work below.

The Mordiford Wyvern

Picture a girl   as she carefully clutches
her blackberry bag   on a morning's stroll
in the night deep woods.   The only sounds
are a leaf's fall   and the shadows reaching.
At the foot of a tree   she finds strange treasure:
an infant serpent,   abandoned and breathful.
She cups it, warms it   and pockets the creature.
Hidden from mother   and father, she fetches it
meat scraps and   scraping bone,
milk sops and mint   and sings it to sleep
in the blackberry bag   under her bed.

Time passes.   The creature, now brawny
and fitfully wild,   cannot be contained
so they leave in the night   and creep to the ridge
that looks down on the woods.   'I'll return', she says,
and she does, next day,   with a whole leg of mutton.
For the first time   she sees him, full grown
and steel-limbed,   with the head of a dragon,
the tuberous tongue   taking flight from the jaws,
and the skin wings a canopy,   straining the sun.
Turning her back,   she flees from the scene
and returns to the arms   of her suffering mother.

Weeks pass, rain falls.   The talk in the village
is of livestock missing   and a path to the woods
now spoiled with blood.   A few brave farmers
ride up to the ridge;   they return in silence,
horseless. Now   a hero is sought
to dispatch the dragon,   with nothing to lose
and no life left to live.   A desperate criminal,
spared from the noose,   is chosen and armed.

Viper-wine drunk,   he follows the trail
to the lair of the beast.   The serpent is sleeping.
He raises his sword,   takes aim at the neck.
From the shadows beyond   a woman emerges
and throws him a bag -   'Leave him be!' she begs.
The creature is stirring.   She pleads in the moonlight;
he turns and runs home   with the bag at his side.
'Did you kill it?' they demand: In the bag is a tongue
from some dreaded brute   (or so it would seem).
'The deed, it is done!';   the criminal released.

The killings cease   and the blood goes to earth.
The girl is still walking   with her blackberry bag
through the silent woods.   Look up, when the sun
seems to fade and falter: you might see a cloud,
immense but fleet,   or a shadow made of wings.

Father and Child Lamp

In the corner, near the piano,
there's a standard lamp;
the father, straight-backed,
smart gold, and the child,
a flexible miniature of Dad,
clutched to his puffed-out chest.

The child beams his yolk eye
at watercolours in plain frames,
or, occasionally, makes the ivory
shimmer on the keys.

Father is in darkness - spark
out some time ago. Now,
his head collects insects
and dust. The bulb, irreplaceable,
shorts out, declines to illuminate.

But he still holds his child close,
his seeing-eye in the shadows.

The Synesthesia Procedure

I'm undergoing the complete procedure,
glitches, they said, in the old grey matter

now they've shaved me and wheeled me into the theatre
masked and tooled-up as they watch me slip under

so blossom sounds just like a choir singing
thunderstorms taste of old silver fillings

Friday is grey but Sunday's magenta
peppermint sounds like pawed sandpaper

one to a hundred's a wooden staircase
verbs smell of vinegar but nouns have no taste

guitar solos swirl into typhoons of staves
and the blood melody pulses through my veins

as I come around, objects start to resolve
at first it's a shock, or so I've been told

everything is familiar, but different somehow
when I smell the word 'flower' I smell the word flower

Loch Fyne

No stars above Loch Fyne tonight -
the clouds have not consented.

The Milky Way, that should rent
the skies undone, hangs somewhere;

we are left with a useless black lint.
Be content, then, with your single malt,

the colour so redolent of amber,
you expect a prehistoric midge

to fix in its trap of fumes.
The unblinking stare of the munros

across the loch is almost spent
and the tousled swell of the water

can only offer the clouds'
reflection back up to heaven.

5 Poems about the Isle of Sheppey

1. Sheerness

whoever said
              no man is an island
had not seen the gentleman
                       exiting
the Wine Store in Sheerness
this morning

shock-haired with yellowing skin
              knotted across his face
like canvas on the wings of a Wright Brothers plane
crazed eyes like black cherries
                rolling around in bone cups
pink short-sleeved shirt/blue shorts
and a white baseball cap. He
twitched spastically
              speaking in tongues
to his bottle of knocked-down gin

what were they saying to each other?
no-one came near enough to hear
         him
the crowd moved about the man like current
around an island,
              hurrying on their way to
somewhere more like
home

2. Minster Leas

Here is a photographic composition,
divided into three distinctive bands.

First, the estuarine expanse of water
that spreads out before you; Holland on the right
and Southend to the left. It is the autopsy
grey of the morgue. The sea conceals the dead -
shells, wrecks and memories of a land mass
that shelved out further before it gave up
and caved in. To swim in it is to self-harm,
except there won't be a ladder of cuts
to wear as a badge to the club later.

Then, there is the ineptly-pebbled beach
that holds fast to the land's cruel gradient.
The beach is a gauntlet thrown down, a challenge
to enjoy; spread a towel, try your luck.
At low tide, it reveals its treasure chest
of hexagonal insects and palsied seaweed.
The sand extends so far you could see yourself
walk to Clacton, or the proprietary windmills
that secure the horizon. As the Moon
drags up the last of the Thames, your escape
route vanishes with a tide that hisses
and the night buries your dreams in scurf.

Finally, the broad and level promenade
of cafés and warning signs that stretches
from cliffs to the swollen concrete lip,
a sea wall, that runs around Sheerness,
protecting the populace from the seaview
(or vice versa). The promenade offers solace
in the shape of benches, every thirty
feet or so. Occasionally, there's a bronze
plate, inscribed with a dead loved one - how he
loved this bench, how she loved this view. A few
sport fresh flowers, withstanding the salt-breeze
long enough to keep their rouges and pinks.

So, then: come sit with the dead on the Leas,
swallow a deep salt breath and take it all in.

3. Bluetown

A street in Bluetown, flanked
by a mile-high wall. We parked
up and took in the view. There was:

a sex-shop, decked out in
labial pink and 3 a.m.
black, with descriptions

of what you find inside.
Next to it: a public house
for sailors, with a wedding

reception - the bride and groom,
spoiling, but in good heart,
nevertheless. And finally:

a heritage centre, got up like a music-hall
from the past - an ark of culture saved
for the nation. It was shut.

Conception, marriage
and old age - life as a street.
We leave, soon after.

4. The Ballad of Ann Plott

'At least one miracle is credited to Minster. At some time (the date seems to have been lost in the telling and re-telling of the story) a year-old child called Ann Plott who lived in a cottage nearby was run over by a loaded dung-cart and crushed 'flat as a pancake'. A passing woman led prayers for the child, who miraculously returned to life and actually spoke her mother's name for the first time as she did so. Before night fell the same day, the child was dancing in the street again, evidently tempting fate to send another dung-cart to do the same thing all over again'

http://minster-kent.kentpoi.co.uk/

'Flat as a pancake' they said that she was.
Truth was, she been concussed, is all.
Hit by the dung-cart on its way through our town,
the horse was disturbed and ran her straight down;
she cracked her head nearly upright with the fall.

She was only a year on God's brownish earth
when fate and shit crossed paths with Ann Plott.
Dancing and singing with never a worry,
she tempted the fates; we prayed for His mercy
as mother rained tears on the now-empty cot.

The afternoon passed and the doctor was called;
he left us in silence with nothing but pain.
The crowd had disbanded, they had turned away
when a miracle happened: we heard the word 'May'.
Ann Plott had risen and spoke her mum's name!

The crowd had returned, the mother was rapt;
how had Ann woken from death's easy grip?
The cart-driver sang as he stood by his horse;
we hugged her, thankful. It could have been worse;
we'd nearly lost Ann just one year from the crib.

Later that day, when the joy had resumed
and the street had been cleared of the accident previous,
you'd find little Ann with a skip in her step,
with a song in her soul you'd be foolish to stop
and a newly-found voice to sing it melodious.

But you'd have to look closer to notice the differences:
the mum at the door with her arms folded tighter,
the looks on the faces of townsfolk who pass
by the girl who still dances dead set in the path
of the dung-cart that's approaching sooner or later.

5. Minster Abbey Gatehouse Museum

Seaxburh, '*of Six Districts*',
Saxon ex-Queen of Kent,
rematerializes on the site
of her Benedictine
nunnery in Minster,
on the Isle of Sheppey.

A fine rain, clarified
by weak sunshine, dampens
her couvrechef. Why she
is here is a mystery
(but it's not the weather).
She surveys the scene from

the highest vantage point
of the island. To the
west, where the sun has set,
are the familiar marshes,
home to emerald swathes
of Samphire or Sampire,

or *herb de Saint Pierre* -
the boys called it Pickleweed -
that she and her daughter
Eormenhild used to pick;
snap the new buds off and
eat it raw, a vegetal

straw that sucks the saltwater
up through its roots. But now
there's a bridge, a thrown rope
that holds back the island
from floating away with
the tide. And so many

dwellings around this hill!
An army encampment,
arranged for an assault?
The thick of night is coming;
this is no place to dwell.
She makes for the gatehouse,

catching sight of the cars
in the park, the police van,
parked up. Lead, as was then,
is still a currency
and the young learn to rob
before they can walk, round

this way. As she's climbing
the stairs, she rises through
history. There is her
family tree, hanging
up on the wall - father Anna,
son of Eni, her husband

Eorcenberht and her sisters
Æthelburg and Saethryth -
but written in a foreign
hand. The next floor, a pageant
of faces stare from the walls
like ghosts. The dust's still

here, though. Finally, she
breaks through to the rooftop.
In the flimsy darkness,
the Isle is a sea of lights
surrounded by slate. She
sways at the thought of all

she has seen, the royalty
she once was when she was
Queen of Kent. Only memory
keeps her here now, on this
island, and the industry
of this museum. She

exists despite the tyranny
of the now, the new. She
vanishes as soon as
the moon rises, only
to return again, same
opening time, tomorrow.

A Dialogue in Tanka
between Eugene Cernan and the Moon

Eugene Cernan:

So many years have passed
since we travelled through the stars
together, it seems.
On Earth, we are rooted; the high
branches barely clear our heads.

The Moon:

The Earth looks peaceful
as if a drop of water
had frozen in mid-air.
It is how I imagine
a child's clear face reflects me.

Eugene Cernan:

Before I left you,
I spelt out my daughter's name
in the dust of you.
In return, I drew your face
on a page in her diary.

The Moon:

So many of you
arrived and planted your flags –
I was not prepared.
My seas had long since run dry
and my days were endless nights.

Eugene Cernan:

When I close my eyes
I see your bright O peer out
of trees and oceans.
As I let go of life, so
I leave the Earth to join you.

The Moon:

The path that you take
is an old one.
Do not fear;
there are stars to point the way.
As you hold me in your memory,
I hold onto your footprints.

Memory Cento

An elderly man fell off his horse
in crossing a ford on a winter's night;
open the head, taking the brains,
wash, pick and cleanse.

When it is injured, remembrance
is impaired; salt, pepper and parsley
the seat of memory, chop the brains fine,
put bye in a cloth.

Ever afterward he could not bring
to his recollection the names of
his wife and children: one was called Facey,
the other Diamond,

and the third, Oblivion, the Child of Cold.
Facey so thin, the wind would have blown
her away; sever out the bones,
cut the skin (all her flesh

was gone). She stared out of her great eyes
as though she'd seen a ghost -
at other times, words beginning with a vowel
cannot be found.

What was more, the fireplace in the kitchen
was one great pile of wood-ash; clean
the pot very clean or it will burn too.
His bad memory

fell from a considerable height
upon his head. He was bothered with it;
he could not see how all this had come about.
One morning he went

into his cowshed, and there he found his
sweet herbs pulverized, although he did not
cease to recognise and love them as
fondly as before.

Matters

Opening the drawer of my father's desk
one childhood morning, I found this

box - it was gun-metal grey
with ballpoint scribble, faded away.

Inside, an air pistol, cocked, not loaded.
Instructions, handled, but carefully folded

around the barrel. I barely touched it
before replacing the ill-fitting lid.

One pack of thumbtacks - brass Os,
turning on their magnetic toes,

in a plastic carton the colour of opal.
A ruler - wooden, of the old school -

metric one side, then imperial;
the inches felt prouder. There were spirals,

compass points, geometric glyphs
on the width; a reassuring grip.

Seven pounds, roughly, in loose change -
florins, shillings, pieces of eight -

and a five pound note, broad as my hand,
blue as heaven, flat as land.

And that was it, save empty spaces.
What had been there, removed in haste

or maybe there was more to come?
Pushing it shut, I left the room

with something of his: a memory
of precious things and stationery.

Jupiter and the Moon

This morning,
I saw the Moon,
punched into the sky,
and Jupiter, subordinate
yet vast beyond reason,
by its side.

And I felt
much as that ancient man
must have felt
as the impact of the car crash
made birds fly
out of his mouth.

A blue dress with a yellow bow

My daughter has asked me to choose her a dress
this morning. I thumb through the rack in her closet
and hooked, by its sleeves, is this blue checked dress, tied
back with a yellow bow. This will do; she accepts

and then leaves. In her room, I consider this
contrast: the father I am and the father
I thought I would be. Forty years back and I'm
playing with plastic cocktail sticks at Grandad's;

swords for a dolls' house duel. There are blue, yellow,
green ones there. This was the sitting room where the cold
had settled. No vistors: no heating. I lay,
flat, in the deep carpet of the afternoon.

Some spikes have pub signs: Red Lion, White Hart, and
The Bricklayer's Arms with its sawdust for stardust;
there's a Polaroid, capturing my Grandad
there, bagging a plain woman, grinning at the flash.

My cocktail sticks catch in the eyes of the Axminster;
pulling them out makes them hook more fiercely.
In the front room, my father and his father
smoke roll-ups from a Golden Virginia tin,

with the racing on. I'm excluded from all this
by the fug of adultness. But they, too, must
be separate from my world of symbols and swords
and the trains as they drift past the gasometer husks

outside. Eventually I became all they were -
tobacco and betting, Directors and Teachers,
and more. I spelled out the iconography of maleness,
took a woman to bride and made a daughter.

I reason, then, I made it to their room. Now
I am here: forcing myself to wonder how
there's no smoke drifting, but lazily hanging so
is a light blue cotton dress, backed with a yellow bow.

Supermarket Boy with Carts, Memphis 1965
(from a photograph by William Eggleston)

1

She comes each morning to watch him
collect carts in the parking lot.
She doesn't buy anything;
her wallet is empty. An only son
away in Vietnam; *Mint Juleps*
and the television stars for company.

2

He wants a cherry-red convertible
and a girl who will. The carts
are cages; he, too, will be trapped
by money and time, eventually.
But, for now, there is always
his dream, his Dream.

3

Two shadows on the store wall:
mother and son reunited or
his dinner, straight from the oven.

The Pinchfist

He flicked switches, brought darkness into rooms
because he could. He was plagued by a mania
for money-saving; sewed scraps of paper
together to make note-pads, kept peelings
in a margarine tub on the kitchen windowsill
and turned the colour down on the TV set
to spare the tube. He bought his wife a mink coat
but it stayed in its box to minimise wear and tear.
When she died, there was no need for light at all;
he sat in front of a blank screen, reflecting
on nothing. The leavings went straight in the bin,
along with the coat. He had learnt the hard way
there was nothing, in time, that could be saved.

December Night

The moon
is made
of gold.

It brushes
against the cheek
of night;
somewhere,
a pulse
quickens.

We sleep
above the sun,
trapping its warmth
in space
between the curve
of your back, the curve
of my chest.

Outside,
water freezes
in stalks holding
up spent
flower heads.

A fox breathes
in starlight,
exhales frost that
waits in the shadows
all morning for our
footfall.

Roots

She wouldn't leave his grave;
the rain soaked the wild grass about her feet
as the wind tugged the orange lilies from his vase
and flung them into the carpark beyond.
But, still, she wouldn't walk away.

He'd waited for her with the engine idling, once,
scratching parallel nail lines into the steering wheel.
She arrived late, bags crammed with shoes
and clothes he'd never let her wear.

They got home, argued. She smashed a plate
so he gave her a baby without her consent.

Today, she waited on him; scraped the dirt
from his name with a red fingernail.
If she had more money, she would have fed
the parking meter, too. Back home,

she arranged her wet things in the hall,
poured herself a glass of sparkling wine
and went upstairs to cover up her roots.

The Dedicated Seat

Did you sit here every evening ? Or only
when the warm days came in early May?
The sun was low behind the village church,
a shadow-spire thrown across the cricket pitch
and the daisies that followed the boundary, not yet cut.

You loved this seat, the view it came with, more;
the legend on a brass plaque says as much.
Did you know the old concrete seat, over there,
had engulfed itself with nettles? Did you eye
the pub that shut six months ago, one night,

and never opened again? And those clouds
that hover above the hills across the valley -
were they yours, too? So many birds, so many songs;
magpies, casting for worms, and the pigeons
('rats with wings') you cursed all summer long.

Did the fleet mayflies dab at your face
as the London flightpaths crossed above
your head? You loved it here, it's clear enough,
under the oak buds set hard against
the watercolourist's blue. You loved it more

when there was cricket to watch, with nothing
but a lost kite's trail of bunting-coloured runners,
glutting the lane above the village green,
to take your eye off the ball - the arc
of the bowler's arm, the release to earth.

Had you put your tomatoes in by now or
had the frosts not left your garden of the night?
There's nobody left to tell me. Just this seat
of yours, the view and the evening sun, and
the dedication of your memory to this place.

A Moon on my Pillow

One day in summer, I reached up through
the clouds and, carefully, took the moon
as it was moving. I pulled it to my chest,
hiding it so no-one would notice, then
ran home and hid it under my bed. Later
that night, after supper, when it was proper-
-ly dark, I took the moon out to examine it.
The surface felt like pumice stone or sticky
bone, cold but with a promise of warmth.
I ran my fingertips over the craters, smooth
ravines and jagged valleys. Moon dust caught
between my fingerprints like broken chalk
and the tiny mist of its atmosphere
drifted across my palms. Seas spread clear
and white upon their shores like quicklime.
It seemed at once ancient, as infinite as time,
then a child, waiting to grow up and push
away on its own. Feeling guilty, I took
the moon and placed it on the pillow next
to me, fell deep asleep and dreamt
of cheese and stone ghosts. Next morning,
thinking that my dreams were like a warning
I took the moon, wrapped it in a bedsheet,
tiptoed down the stairs, gently eased
the kitchen door and stepped outside. I climbed
the ladder propped against the washing line
and, on tiptoe, put the moon back in orbit.
It set off again like a wound-up clock, tick-
-ing away in the sky as if nothing had happened.
That night, it rose above the woods beyond
my house and hovered at my window, longer
than the moon should. I hid beneath the sheets
hoping it would not part the clouds and come for me.

Digging a Grave

The lush cemetery grass, the dead's roof,
is where you begin. At dawn, look
for a pleasing aspect within touching
distance of yew trees, shrubs. Mark out
a man-sized oblong with cooking twine,
shave the sods and file neatly in lines.
Dig down: your spade bites through clay,
stone shards, clay pipes, dogs' teeth
and the like. The sun will shift above you
but, today, you will set before it does.
Down, down through the ages until you feel
the earth's fingers clutch at your heels.
Spread the floor with autumn's leaves
or sawdust, then climb the ladder out
of the grave mouth's yaw. Line the sides
with butchers' grass and sweep the dirt away.
All that's left is wait to fill it up again;
your soil, your work and the life you made.

Branch Lines

My finger travelled it first;
along the notched line,
like a stitched-up wound,
from where the walk resumed
to the public house sign.

It cut between the trees
with engineer's precision;
a disused railway track,
raised and cross-hatched
with leaves. We stopped to listen

to the silence. Above,
a fog was held in place
by sycamore canopies
like the steam released
from long-departed trains.

As a boy, I saw one once
from a platform. Nothing
stopped me from reaching out,
touching it as it passed. How
I felt like I was dreaming!

The iron shriek of brakes
and the engine as it slowed
like a vast beetle, cloaked
in iron and sulphurous smoke,
and only my buttoned-up duffle-coat

to protect me. Today, those trains,
into their own night, have passed.
Figures from yesterday once
regarded these trees through
sepia windows in Second-Class;

now they see only their own
reflections. Men came and ripped
out the tracks that never crossed
and sold them off at a loss.
The engines rust with only bits

of broken coaches for company.
Behind, the sun strengthens,
sending our shadows home;
they mark out tracks for ghosts
of journeys past as they lengthen.

He listens to photocopiers

can read signs and texts
in their chugs, clunks

like resting an ear
on a train track or,
crouched on the pacific shore,

eavesdropping on whales
singing love
to each other.

He tunes into
the rhythm of print lore;
of double-sided, stapled A4

as it fetches, falls,
catches, releases and,
finally, brushed to a standstill,

lies, raw, in the finishing tray.
And, as with his attempts
at flirting, he knows

that what he puts in
will emerge the same -
only more so.

The Soft Whip

Was it exhaust, or the metallic tang
of the soft whip from the ice-cream van?
Had one not pulled up by my house today,
I wouldn't be sitting here in middle age,
closing in on my childhood again,
still trying to pin that sensation down:
taste or scent, or false memory
of the sweet white smack of counterfeit cream
as the man in the van circled the cone
beneath the nozzle to collect his foam.
I was handed a sculpture; its waves
and folds ran smooth and bladed,
the symmetry spoilt by a flake, stuck
in the thick. The engine ran, its fumy chug
powering the fridge and occasional chimes
of *Greensleeves*, a few bars at a time
from a tin-can speaker. I handed the change
I had with my spare hand and made
to walk home but stopped for a lick,
seconds from the first oily trickle
to trace my knuckles. And the taste?
It was petrol, blossom and vegetable fat,
milk teeth and forecourts, and tarmac
that never set but stuck to your sole
in those infinite summers of all
school holidays at once when I sang
all I could see before the school bell rang.

The Great Attractor

Through the contrails
that hatch and spread,
and the tungsten fog
above the rooftops,

you might see
a gathering of stars
tonight. Kill the lights
and catch Orion's Belt;

a miniature garden of
milky-white flowers
budding the peat of night.
Hidden behind the curtain,

the Great Attractor
flashes his pearly-whites,
waiting for his moment
on the red carpet.

Wednesday, At the Bible Meeting

'Dylann Roof, 21…spent an hour in Bible study with parish-
ioners at the nearly 200-year-old Emanuel African Methodist
Church before opening fire on them'

Reuters, 19/6/2015

*'Therefore, if anyone is in Christ, he is a new creation, the old
has gone, the new has come'*

Corinthians 5:17

A young white gentleman has entered
our Church; he pushes through the doors,
letting in a slant of late evening sunlight
and a handful of jasmine flowers that,
briefly, pool in the lobby.

He walks up the aisle and sits with us,
but apart. Our topic for tonight
is forgiveness. We are considering
Corinthians 5:17; *all are forgiven
who are in Christ.* This church,

I think, is like a vessel of His love;
red decked, white hulled with
wooden balconies to hold
His celestial crew. We set course,
with purpose, for the Promised Land;

neither the mighty earthquake nor
the fires of men can dispute
our course! Our visitor
shifts on his bench, his hands
tucked protectively under his jeans.

Eye-contact does not come freely
to him; he stares at the carpet
but he is listening, at least. New
blood, and from outside the arms
of our community, is always

55

welcome. The Pastor speaks of
redemption and sin; the young man
glances at the exit then slowly
up to the easy brilliance of
the chandeliers, as if unsure of

which offers the absent comfort
he craves. His face returns
to his intensive study of the floor;
unblinking, uninhibited.
Time was when this church

built a revolt. Sedition burned
in our hearts and eyes;
a righteous vengeance to defy
and rectify the eternal wrongs
that the White Man had visited

upon us in His name
and their commerce. The flame
faltered and change came slower
than the fires that once burnt
this church to naught. Change

has not come yet; but anything
is better than nothing. And what
does this young visitor signify?
That we are free to associate? His
separateness jars; his dress and his

manner say he is here but he is
not here, also. He looks over his
shoulder at the entrance as if to
pace out the steps of his leaving,
which will be presently. In the

Slave Market museum nearby, there is
an illustration, for the benefit of
Slaveowners, on how to whip a
pregnant slave face down so as not
to blight (devalue) the unborn

(future slave): dig a pit to hold the
swell of the belly, it instructs.
I wept when I saw it first, and
I still weep now when I recall the
purity of that conception of evil.

Tonight, I mentally imprint
the face of the unseen slaver upon
that of the young white man
seated among us; it does not seem
out of place, after all these years.

And then the Pastor calls for us to
share. There is a pause, and the
White Man stands and reaches
into his jacket pocket. But, as bibles
fall to the floor and pews are tipped

backwards, it is clear from
his face - has always been there
from the start - that he has already shown
us what he has to offer, under the
fractured lights of the grand chandelier

above.

Missing

The notice told he'd gone away, was lost in France
(you half-knew the truth but prayed he hadn't fallen
to mustard gas or trapped by wire in No Man's Land).

Our boy has crossed the sea, it said, to fight the Hun,
not long out of short pants, a summer shy of nineteen;
so are we desirous for particulars of our only son.

What did you expect? A sighting of a man who could
be him now fighting in another regiment or mending
in a Kentish house, all memory of who he once was

buried in French mud that was a French wood once?
You listened but no word came. Hope faded fast
and every fallen leaf a name appended to the civil list.

He never made it back or even out the ranks. He gave
his life up for the flag but his story passes down the years
so men might learn that lines on maps are only lines on maps.

A name in stone has fixed his place in history. Your fingertips
can read each letter. The dust the chisel made has scattered
but still brings tears when the wind blows from the East.

The Thin Place

is a bridge with no span
  cells dividing inside a beach tan
  the thickness of a coffin lid
  a word's echo, caught in an ear
  a final breath, ex haled
  the bloom on a rotting apple
  what separates sap from bark
shows beneath the roots
  of a storm-bowed oak

is a cigarette paper blackening
  a snowflake on a knuckle, melting
  forensic dust on fingerprints
  balloons blown to bursting point
  a Venn diagram of love and lust
  a wingtip emerging from Autumn mist
clipping the cathedral spire
  with one engine still turning, one lost

Winter Solstice

Why has the sun stopped here?
Caught by a hard frost
in a notch made of stone,
it could be penned, or snared
with rope and bone. Perhaps
the sound the livestock made
when slaughtered last night
gave it pause. The screams
were still caught in the trees
this morning like wet leaves.
Was it hunger, then? Of meat,
we have plenty; nothing else
grows here this time of year
but nails and shadows. We light
fires against the longest night
and fill the air with smoke
and words. Our figures play
against the sarsens as if
we were dancing; nothing
to be gained from standing still.

Black Hellebore

When the sun can barely drag itself
above the horizon, blown as it is
with the corpses of dead and blasted fruit,

you appear through the sunken foliage,
the mass graves of the summer.
They name you the Christmas Rose

and say you were made from the tears
of a girl who had no gift for Christ.
But you are gift enough; snow angel

with a heart made of sunlight. They say
you induce vertigo and swell the tongue;
it is the price we pay for unearned beauty.

Once, they even blessed their animals
in the confetti of your petals, and kept
a witch or two at bay with your poison.

Small wonder, then, that they know not
what to make of you; pink-tinged intruder,
the bell that sounds at night by the headstone.

Father

'The child is the father of the man',
William Wordsworth

In the beginning, you laughed at everything.
You rubbed your heels together to make blood
soak the blankets in the cot. Dreaming

of milk and cats, you pissed in arcs
and woke up, wet. Then, you held
buttercups under chins, killed wasps,

dug holes, swam like a starfish, climbed
apple trees. Soon, you grew up fast and thin,
fought in meadows, told black and white lies,

spoke to Diana the moon at night,
lost teeth, kicked balls against the pricks
and told the Speaking Clock to go fuck itself.

Much later, in the golden age of cigarettes,
you smiled at the girls with Pepsi-blue eyes
in the Coke-black dark, smirked at Christ

in a Welsh church, pissed money up walls
and watched it fall. You left me with little to show
for those years of front and fireworks.

And I watch you now as you shave in the mirror
for no-one, wondering why you let slip all that
incandescent energy as it seeps down through

the floorboards to settle with the dead
skin, tears, clippings and stardust.
I want to grab your shoulder, then

tell you I'm lost without you. *Dad, look here,*
I say; *I want you back, I don't know what to do
since there's nothing left to laugh at anymore.*

62

Hestia/Mother

You were there before me;
we had no choice.

In a clearing of the forest,
with the night caught
in the branches, we make a fire.

My father builds a pyramid
of kindling; I stare the stars down,
but their antiquity stuns me.

At once there is light and sound;
the crack to attention, the embrace.
We sit and absorb the affection,

safe in our shared fortune.
Your warmth is as familiar
as once was your face. But

where we were, where we are going,
is of no consequence now; there is only
here, in our circle of trees.

Your smoke rises in your absence.
The trees point to your home;
it is a clearing in the darkness,

between constellations,
where you journey on another path.
My father and I, we both know

you were there before us;
we have no choice.

ARENIG PRESS
Dolfawr
Cwmrheidol
Aberystwyth
Ceredigion
SY23 3NB

www.arenig.co.uk